DUBAI
A PICTORIAL TOUR

MOTIVATE
PUBLISHING

DUBAI

A PICTORIAL TOUR

Published with the support and encouragement of
Dubai Chamber of Commerce & Industry

غرفــة دبــي
DUBAI CHAMBER

Published by Motivate Publishing

Dubai: PO Box 2331, Dubai, UAE
Tel: (+971 4) 282 4060, fax: (+971) 4 282 0428
e-mail: books@motivate.ae   www.booksarabia.com

Office 508, Building No 8, Dubai Media City, Dubai, UAE
Tel: (+971 4) 390 3550, fax: (+971) 4 390 4845

Abu Dhabi: PO Box 43072, Abu Dhabi, UAE
Tel: (+971 2) 677 2005, fax: (+971) 2 677 0124

London: Acre House, 11/15 William Road, London NW1 3ER
e-mail: motivateuk@motivate.ae

Directors: Obaid Humaid Al Tayer
                      Ian Fairservice

Consultant Editor: David Steele
Deputy Editor: Moushumi Nandy
Assistant Editor: Zelda Pinto
Art Director: Andrea Willmore
Senior Designer: Cithadel Francisco

General Manager Books: Jonathan Griffiths

© Motivate Publishing 1996, 1999, 2002 and 2007

First published 1996
Reprinted 1997
Second edition 1999
Reprinted 2000
Third edition 2002
Fourth edition 2007

ISBN: 978 1 86063 168 9

British Library Cataloguing-in-Publication Data. A catalogue record for this
book is available from the British Library.

Printed by Rashid Printers & Stationers LLC, Ajman, UAE

INTRODUCTION

From His Highness Sheikh Hamdan bin Rashid Al Maktoum, Deputy Ruler of Dubai,
UAE Minister of Finance and Industry and Chairman of Dubai Municipality

If you are new to Dubai, welcome – and I hope this book will serve as a useful introduction. And for residents, or visitors who are already familiar with the emirate, I believe it will present some perspectives of our country and history that you may not have seen before.

For those who have recently arrived I suggest that, to get a feel for the place and to begin to understand how and why it works, you take a stroll along the Creek. Appropriately, the waterway features prominently in this book, simply because it has featured prominently in our history. The activities that occur on and around it are, in essence, a microcosm of the whole, industrious, multicultural, adaptable and tolerant city.

The Creek curves through Dubai, its waters reflecting ancient windtowers and neon advertisements, its skyline alternately punctuated by slender minarets and high-rise offices. Moored at its wharves or churning its surface are trading dhows and fishing boats, pleasure craft and *abras*. Elegant hotels and handsome gardens line its banks, while the walls of the merchants' houses in the old quarter are still lapped by its tides. Busy along its shores are the people of many nations who live and work here – bringing a cultural variety that enriches every aspect of life in the city.

Geography, of course, has helped. Dubai, positioned midway between Europe and the Far East, is at the hub not only of the wealthy Middle East but of a much greater market that stretches from the Levant to the Indian subcontinent and from the newly emerging states of the CIS to Africa. But then, throughout the world, strategic locations, especially seaports, have historically been centres of trading activity – although not all have taken full advantage of their position by developing trading skills and supporting services, nor have they all attracted commerce and industry. Those that have – and the most notable examples are Hong Kong and Singapore – have the added ingredient of a liberal regulatory system.

Here in Dubai – while we have, of course, necessary controls and legislation sufficient to secure a fair and just commercial environment – the authorities prefer to leave companies to get on with what they do best: running their businesses.

Dubai has always been ready to trade, and to invest in an infrastructure that has already attracted so much commerce and industry to the emirate – ports and cargo facilities, accommodation and telecommunications, modern road systems, airports and an award-winning airline.

In addition to the benefits offered by the city itself, the free zones at Jebel Ali, Dubai International Airport, Dubai International Financial Centre, Dubai Internet City, Dubai Media City and elsewhere, have been specifically designed to provide a congenial environment for business. And the needs of the people who live and work here have been equally carefully considered and catered for by the provision of ancillary services, ranging from education to entertainment, sports and leisure facilities to hospitals and clinics, high-quality housing (with expatriates having the right to purchase property on a freehold basis in certain developments) and ease of access for travellers and goods.

While Dubai's history can be traced back some 6,000 years, there has been more change in the last four decades than in the whole of the preceding six millennia. Even as recently as the early 1950s Dubai was still a small entrepôt trading port, the occupants of which, since the decline of the pearl trade a generation earlier, had returned to earning a modest living from the import and re-export of goods.

Then, the regular P&O steamships from Bombay would anchor a mile offshore, their cargoes and passengers being unloaded and brought to land by small boats of sufficiently shallow draught to enable them to enter the Creek. And at the desert airstrip the occasional DC3, Heron and Dove would whisk up the sand on the unpaved runways. Few people then could anticipate what immense changes would take place in the years ahead.

But one man could: His Highness Sheikh Rashid bin Saeed Al Maktoum, whose sons Sheikh Maktoum and Sheikh Mohammed have so ably continued our late father's policies, combining the shrewdness and trading skills of a merchant with the foresight and imagination of a visionary. If you would like to see his monument then stand at any vantage point in Dubai and look around – not just at the buildings themselves, although they are impressive enough – but also at the people, the activity and the way of life: together they form a unique and still-developing testament.

Hamdan bin Rashid Al Maktoum

The Emirates occupies the southern shores of the Arabian Gulf, where the vast expanse of the Rub al-Khali – The Empty Quarter (left) – extends for more than 1,000 kilometres across the Arabian Peninsula. Much of the country's 78,000 square kilometres consists of sand desert, with the dunes reaching heights of 100 metres or more in some parts. The dunes are in constant motion, being blown across the landscape at an average rate of 60 centimetres per year. *Jebels* (mountains) tower over the plains throughout the interior of the United Arab Emirates, offering stark evidence as to the power of the earth's shifting tectonic plates (above). They have been home to Arabia's settled tribal people for aeons. Although the UAE has been in existence only since 1971, the country's geology and topography have revealed much about its past and the land is rich in fossils.

9

With rain falling on 10 days a year on average, life was harsh for the Bedouin who roamed the hot desert interior as nomads with their camel herds – a way of life that has all but disappeared in the UAE today. Similarly, shepherds and goatherds eked a simple living in the rugged mountains while farmers tended date-palm plantations wherever traces of water could be found.

In the 1830s, a branch of the Bani Yas tribe – led by the Maktoum family – settled on the Shindagha Peninsula at the mouth of the Creek. Under the Maktoums, Dubai became the principal port of the Gulf by the late 1870s. The oldest building in Dubai is Al Fahidi Fort (left). For many years it was the ruler's home and, today, the remarkable fortress endures as a museum celebrating the emirate's Bedouin past. Another venerable building is Sheikh Saeed House (above). Sheikh Saeed bin Maktoum Al Maktoum ruled Dubai from 1912–1958 and lived in this house overlooking the Creek in Shindagha. It is now a fascinating museum and part of an authentic heritage area.

The call to prayer. The houses of Bastikiya offer a haven of tranquillity just a few minutes' walk from several busy souks. Many stand as a testimony to Dubai's architectural heritage, having recently been restored to their original magnificence. Some are open to the public as guest houses, art galleries or restaurants and show how these practical, elegant homes looked in the past.

The Creek (below) succumbed to the same silting process that afflicted other creeks along the Arabian Gulf coast, but it was dredged in the 1960s and this resulted in a surge in cargo volume that soon elevated the town into a major trading hub. Dubai's development included the construction of major road networks. Pictured on the left is Sheikh Zayed Road which, for the first time, provided easy access to Abu Dhabi. It is interesting to compare this 1980s photo with those of today's Sheikh Zayed Road seen on pages 68 and 69.

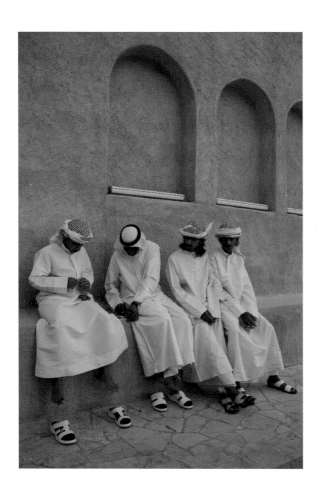

The latter part of the 20th century and the early years of the 21st century have brought changes to the people of Dubai, rocketing them from a simple, nomadic life in the desert to that of players on the international business and technology stage. Even so, national identity remains extremely strong and its continuity is something the local population cherish and are proud to preserve. This is particularly noticeable in the wearing of the white, loose-fitting *kandoura*, the traditional garb for menfolk that is adopted by all generations.

The windtower, an early form of air-conditioning, was introduced to Dubai by the Persians who settled in Bastikiya in the early 20th century. The square towers were divided diagonally to form four triangular shafts and any passing breeze caused air to be pushed down the tower and sucked up again, generating a welcome draught below.

Best visited during holidays and festivals, Dubai's Heritage Village and the adjacent Diving Village in Shindagha are a vibrant living museum to Dubai's heritage and culture. Activities normally start in the late afternoon and include music, dancing and craft activities, while local food is available.

Many dances are performed as part of celebrations, where women swirl their hair and men perform moves that originated as a response to danger, when the tribe would sound their drums and shout before repelling any attack. The spectacle, then as now, presents a fearsome display.

An interesting cross section of local craftspeople can be seen while strolling through Heritage Village. Among others, these include basket weavers and blacksmiths and tinkers who produce some collectable knives that can, of course, be bought as authentic souvenirs of Dubai and Arabia.

Other crafts range from processing cotton by hand to making delicate jewellery, but one of the most popular areas among visitors is the kitchen, where women in colourful dresses and traditional *burqas* (face masks) prepare delicious sweet and savoury pancakes.

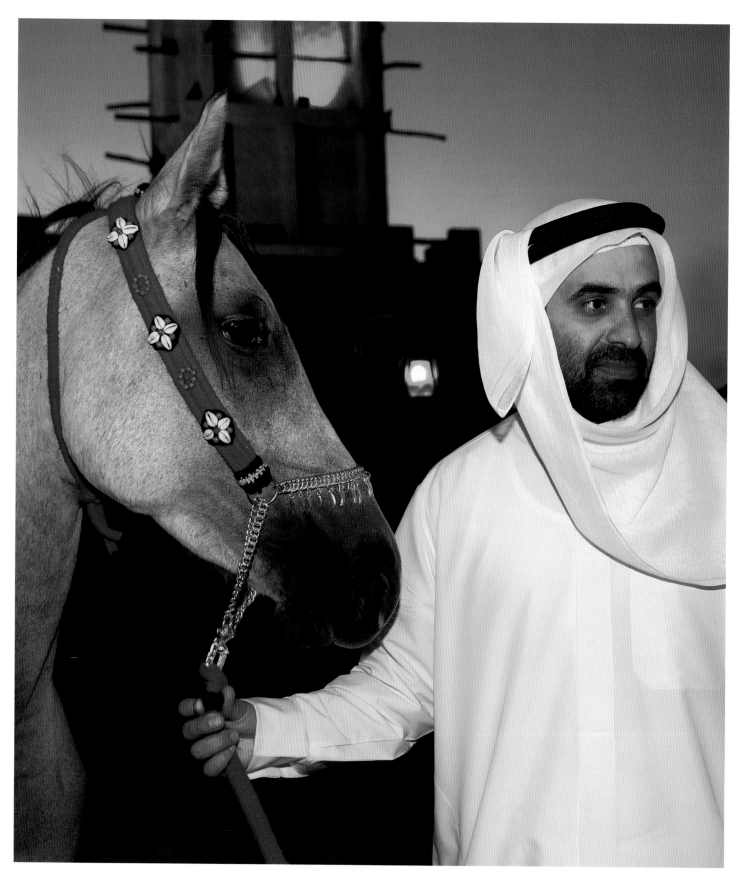

This fine Arabian horse and its master were photographed at Heritage Village, as was this superb windtower – complete with a crescent moon. Elsewhere, this troupe of dancers was relaxing in a *majlis* (meeting place) prior to one of their evening performances.

An elderly Bedouin (left) appears more welcoming than these two guards seen at the Heritage Village (above). Both guards are holding a *jirz* – an Arabian tomahawk normally carried by members of the Shihuh mountain tribe of the Musandam Peninsula situated near Ra's al-Khaimah.

Two men relax in a quiet corner of Heritage Village (above) while visitors to the Diving Village stream past a traditional rowing dhow (right). Races are still regularly held in these long and beautifully made wooden craft.

Falcons are highly prized in the UAE, with top-flight birds being bought and sold for as much as Dhs150,000. The traditional sport of the Emirates, falconry has been the catalyst for numerous developments in avian medicine on a global scale. So intrinsic is the falcon to the nation's psyche that it appears on a number of government agency logos, as well as on the country's currency.

While camels were once an essential ally in the struggle to survive in the desert, many are now largely bred for racing, and good beasts can command extraordinarily high prices. Camels can still be found in large numbers outside the cities and have a propensity for wandering out in front of cars in the middle of highways – a habit that does neither party any good.

Camel-racing attracts huge – and hugely enthusiastic – crowds, whether to the racecourses on the outskirts of the city or to the more informal country circuits, with races of up to 16 kilometres providing a test of stamina as well as speed (right). In contrast to the relaxed exercise scene (above) the start of a race can be chaotic, with camels, riders, trainers and owners occasionally disappearing in the miniature sandstorm created by restless hooves.

Dubai owes much of its prosperity, and indeed its character, to the sea and the trade routes it provided for the city's merchants. But the abundant natural resources of the warm waters of the Gulf also offered other opportunities and traditional racing dhows remain a familiar – and welcome – sight today.

Trade, the source of Dubai's economic strength, is vividly highlighted as you wander round the souks, which provide visitors with first-hand evidence of life in Dubai as it must have been prior to its modern age. The Textile Souk, located adjacent to an *abra* station, provides the visitor with a hint of the rich, redolent bouquet of Arabian heritage. In addition to a huge variety of textiles, other items, including these shoes straight out of *Ali Baba*, are also sold.

Dubai's evocative souks attract visitors from round the world in search of a
bargain. From the Spice Souk in Deira (seen here), to the Gold Souk, Textile Souk
and the new Souk Madinat Jumeirah, it's well worth spending some time
wandering through their alleys with your camera at your side.

Dubai's best-known souk is the Gold Souk. Here, visitors walk through an area of gold glitteringly displayed in the windows of the small shops that line the covered promenade. Many of Dubai's early fortunes were based on the gold trade. Today, the price of gold is fixed daily and items are sold by weight, there being little or no charge for the often exquisite workmanship. As befits the city's high-tech image, an electronic sign at the entrance to the souk displays the current market rate – and each day confirms Dubai as one of the best places in the world to buy this precious metal.

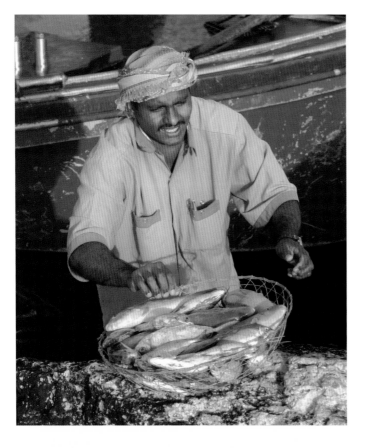

Dubai's residents, accustomed to buying the freshest of fish, flock to the colourful Fish Souk near the mouth of the Creek. Conveniently, meat and a wide variety of vegetables, fruit and dates are also available at this lively marketplace, redolent of the Dubai of earlier times.

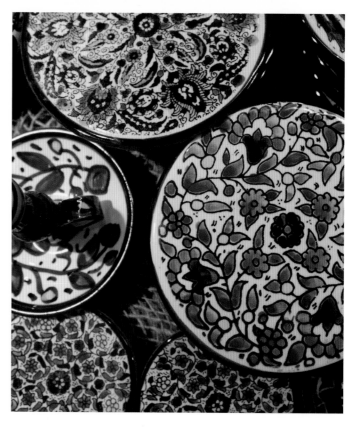

One of Dubai's newer developments is Madinat Jumeirah, set amid nearly four kilometres of waterways along a kilometre of beachfront adjacent to the Burj Al Arab. By using the latest technology, the complex effectively recreates the opulent side of old Arabia and is a remarkable tribute to the emirate's seafaring past and its historical roots as the City of Merchants. It includes the remarkable Souk Madinat Jumeirah seen on these pages as well as a wide variety of restaurants, a popular theatre and an exhibition complex.

Dubai lies at the centre of a global trading crossroads between the east and west and historians believe its Creek, the city's main artery and the reason for Dubai's existence, is probably one of the oldest ports in the world. Today, visitors can take a cruise along the Creek and spy traditional dhows nestled in the shade of the most modern, state-of-the-art, glass-and-chrome buildings.

Dhow crews are tight-knit bands and their vessels become a home from home for months at a time as they ply the ancient trading routes from Dubai to the Indian subcontinent, Iran, Sudan and more distant destinations. A stroll along the creekside, especially in the early evening, will reveal much domestic activity onboard, with tea being brewed, meals being cooked and games being played.

51

Abras have been crossing the Creek for several centuries and remain a popular and inexpensive means of travelling between Bur Dubai and Deira, with a one-way trip costing a dirham from shore to shore. *Abras* can also be hired for private excursions (left). Dubai is a city of exceptional architecture, with soaring chrome-and-glass skyscrapers that mingle seamlessly with the *abras* and traditional wooden dhows, providing a complementary blend of both the ancient and modern Arabia (above and previous spread).

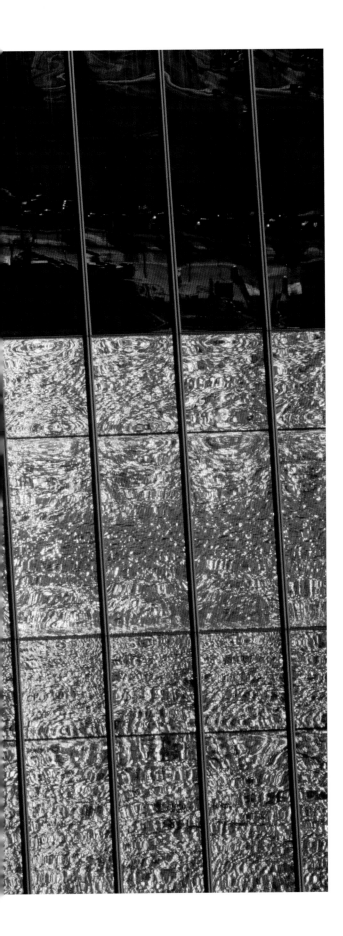

The remarkable National Bank of Dubai Building was designed by Carlos Ott, architect of the Bastille Opera House in Paris. Its curved façade provides interesting reflections of the Creek, especially towards sunset, and it is one of Dubai's most iconic edifices. As seen overleaf, the National Bank of Dubai Building is situated between the Sheraton Dubai Creek Hotel & Towers, on the left, and the blue-glassed Dubai Chamber of Commerce and Industry building.

Sampling *shisha* (aromatic tobacco) and drinking Arabian coffee is a traditional pastime practised in many Dubai restaurants. The Creek's twin towers provide a stunning backdrop to an evening of quiet conversation.

A table with a view: another popular and somewhat unusual culinary experience – especially during the cooler winter months – is dinner aboard one of the many colourful dhow restaurants that ply Dubai Creek.

Dubai has spared no expense in making the city pleasant for its inhabitants, and ongoing projects include the greening of the margins and islands of its road network and the construction of architecturally challenging structures and buildings. Two of the most prominent include Dubai Clock Tower (above), which was built in the mid 1960s on a deserted area of sand close to the Creek, and the Etisalat building (right), one of a number of Etisalat's 'golf-ball' buildings that have become a familiar sight round the country.

Dubai International Airport is situated on the Deira side of the city and has been home to the biannual Dubai Airshow which will be moving to Dubai World Central Airport when it becomes operational. Over the years, Britain's Red Arrows aerobatic team has been a star attraction at the show.

Mankhool (above), is an area of apartment blocks, modern shopping complexes and restaurants. Other popular shopping and dining areas on the Bur Dubai side of the Creek include Karama and Satwa (right).

Today's Dubai is a city of outstanding architecture and boasts one of the best highway networks in the region, linking the city with its neighbours in the UAE and further afield. Soaring skyscrapers mingle side by side with palaces, villas and modern apartment buildings and, as the city has grown, so the urban landscape has expanded. Flyovers, tunnels, highways and bridges have been built, and many more ground-breaking projects are in hand. Dubai's best-known highway, seen on this spread, is Sheikh Zayed Road, which stretches all the way to the city of Abu Dhabi.

The deep faith of the Muslims is embodied in omnipresent mosques, a
fine example of which is the landmark Jumeirah Mosque on Jumeirah
Beach Road (above). Further along Jumeirah Beach Road, zinnias provide
a spectacular carpet of seasonal colour, with Burj Al Arab presenting an
equally stunning backdrop in the distance.

Practically every major hotel chain in the world has a property in Dubai. Many are luxurious resorts, with their own golden sand beaches washed by the warm waters of the Arabian Gulf; while others are conveniently located in the downtown business area of the city. Standards are high and Dubai is one of the very few places in the world that can boast a seven-star hotel – the all-suite Burj Al Arab (left). A spectacular tower that soars to a height of more than 320 metres, it sits on its own island between its sister hotel, the Jumeirah Beach Hotel (previous spread), which is modelled on the shape of a breaking wave, and Madinat Jumeirah (above). All these properties are managed by Jumeirah, Dubai's own international hotel group.

First-class hotels dot the Dubai skyline and guests enter a world where service and luxury are second nature – places where no attention to detail has been spared. There's a culture of prestige, and a devotion to quality and excellence that distinguishes the city from any other in the world. The One&Only Royal Mirage Hotel, seen here, is reminiscent in style of an Arabian palace and offers luxurious interiors with a seductive Arabic ambience and beautifully landscaped grounds facing The Palm Jumeirah.

Dubai Marina was one of Dubai's first developments where people of all nationalities could purchase property. Boasting luxurious residential and leisure facilities, this enormous project is virtually a city within a city; on completion it will be one of the world's largest and most attractive marinas, approximately four and a half square kilometres in size and will have an 11-kilometre boardwalk.

The people of Dubai have a well-earned reputation as dedicated workers and they relish their leisure hours. Children's City Creek Park Dubai (left and below), a unique 'infotainment' facility, offers bright splashes of primary colours set among shades of soothing greenery. Zabeel Park (right), spanning 47.5 hectares, was opened in 2005 and is located at the very heart of Dubai within three distinct zones, interlinked by pedestrian bridges, near the Dubai World Trade Centre. The first technology based park in the Middle East, the recreational area encompasses food courts, an amphitheatre, exhibition centres, a boating lake and a cricket pitch which has quickly become a favourite weekend destination for cricket fans.

Leisure activities are often water-based, ranging from diving and skiing to sailing and kitesurfing. The warm weather, golden beaches and clear waters of the Arabian Gulf are one of Dubai's prime attractions, ensuring the emirate continues to remain popular as a holiday destination and a desirable place to stay for those who enjoy sun, sea, sand and surf.

This spread: The numerous shipwrecks off Dubai have created artificial reefs which have become ideal sites for scuba divers to explore (above). Leisure sailing and ocean racing are also becoming more and more popular, with Dubai even showing a keen interest in the America's Cup (right).

Following spread: This scene of Jebel Ali Beach has a timeless quality. Even in a place changing as rapidly as Dubai, it seems, there are still constants.

Throughout Dubai, the urban landscape is interspersed with parks and gardens. Expanses that were once arid sand have been transformed into verdant oases. One of Dubai's most popular parks is Safa Park, adjacent to Sheikh Zayed Road, which was opened in 1975 and covers an area of 64 hectares. This park is particularly attractive in summer when its flamboyant trees are in bloom – a truly magnificent sight. Here, you may also see or hear ring-necked parakeets. Their loud call is said to be like that of a falcon.

Ski Dubai, said to be the world's largest indoor snow park, is extremely popular with skiers and snowboarders of all ages. With real snow covering an area of 22,500 square metres and with capacity for 1,500 visitors at any one time, this unusual attraction for a hot desert destination boasts five runs of varying difficulties, the longest of which stretches 400 metres.

A happy group of young helpers enjoy a moment at the Dubai Desert Classic. Local and expatriate children feature strongly in daily life and sport in Dubai and enjoy superb educational and recreational facilities. Importantly, they also have a unique opportunity to learn about other nationalities, races and religions, in a relaxed and tolerant environment.

Featuring the region's premier golf courses – and with many new
championship courses being built – Dubai offers the very best in golf in the
Middle East. Although challenging, the courses are varied and, with wide-
ranging tee positions, have been designed for enjoyment, challenging the
world's top professionals while rewarding the weekend and holiday golfer.
Three of the emirate's favourite courses are the Dubai Creek Golf and Yacht
Club (above) with its remarkable clubhouse, The Montgomerie Dubai (top
left) and the Arabian Ranches Golf Club (bottom left).

Dubai boasts the highest international sports profile of all the Gulf cities and, each year, the emirate plays host to many top-notch international sporting events, including the Dubai Desert Classic golf tournament, now a staple of the PGA tour. Regular players include such luminaries as Ernie Els (above) and Tiger Woods (right), both of whom have won the tournament and are closely involved with new golfing developments in Dubai.

Dubai's association with horse-racing is strong and the ruling Al Maktoum family has acquired a formidable reputation, their horses regularly winning some of the most prestigious races on the world calendar. The Emirate offers superb facilities for horses, riders and spectators and is the venue for the world's richest horse race – the Dubai World Cup, held in March. In its short history, the Dubai World Cup has been a spectacular success. Not only has the race drawn many international competitors, it has also been won by some of the world's greatest champion horses, including the legendary Cigar, Singspiel, Silver Charm, Dubai Millennium, Captain Steve and Roses in May. The photo above shows Frankie Dettori winning the race in 2006, riding for the ruling family's Godolphin Stables on Electrocutionist.

Most of the world's top tennis players compete in the annual Dubai Tennis Championships, which were inaugurated in 1993. The male and female championships were dominated between 2003 and 2007 by Roger Federer and Justine Henin, with each player taking the singles title four times.

The popular Dubai Rugby Sevens tournament is a regular winter sporting fixture and typically opens the IRB Sevens World Series, which includes the best Sevens' nations. The tournament attracts thousands of supporters from around the region as well as elsewhere in the world.

Dubai's eclectic range of shopping malls will please even the most blasé of shoppers. Wafi City (above) pays homage to the pharaohs of ancient Egypt. It is an unusual and upmarket mall that offers shops, restaurants and cafés along with a lavish spa and leisure club, set among pyramids, statues, hieroglyphs and cartouches. One of the newest shopping attractions, Dubai Festival City (right), is taking shape next to the Creek, adjacent to the new Business Bay Bridge. A feature of the mall at Dubai Festival City is a variety of cascading waterfalls – one of which is seen here.

Two of Dubai's landmark shopping malls, BurJuman Centre (above) and Mall of the Emirates (right), provide international shopping in lavish surroundings. As well as shops, BurJuman boasts an office tower, high-tech business centre, conference hall, sports facilities and apartments. Mall of the Emirates is the largest shopping mall in the Middle East, although Dubai Mall and Mall of Arabia will take the top spots when they are completed. Mall of the Emirates features more than 400 retailers, 65 restaurants and coffee shops, a 14-screen cinema complex, a theatre and a hotel, but its biggest claim to fame is the Middle East's first indoor ski slope, Ski Dubai.

It may not be the largest shopping complex in Dubai, but Souk Madinat Jumeirah is worth visiting for its vibrant Arabian-bazaar atmosphere in which open-fronted shops, intimate galleries, street cafés and boutique restaurants spill onto paved walkways. Ibn Battuta Mall (right and below), on the other hand, houses 275 outlets and a 21-screen cinema complex – including the UAE's first Imax cinema – and is the largest single-floor shopping mall in the world. It is inspired by the travels of the legendary 14th century Arab explorer of the same name; the photos seen here illustrate Persia and China – two of the many countries Ibn Battuta visited and two of the main regional areas featured in the mall.

Following on the success of the first Christies sale in Dubai – and bringing world-class art to the Emirate – Art Dubai is one of the most eagerly anticipated events on the city's cultural calendar and has become *the* Middle Eastern showcase for the world's top international galleries.

Dining is a popular pastime in Dubai, especially during the cooler winter months. Standards of food and service are all of the highest calibre; whatever the dish and wherever the location. From a taste of Arabia in the souk to casual dining at a themed eatery or a tasty meal in one of the city's Oriental restaurants, the choice of culinary options in Dubai is vast.

Dubai is a multicultural society and the differing interests and activities
of its residents bring colour and variety to every aspect of life. One thing
that's common to all, though, is a liking for the city's exuberant nightlife. As
well as the many opportunities Dubai affords to watch traditional Arabic
entertainment, or enjoy the fun of the fair, there's also a choice of night
clubs and theatres and even the occasional ballet or opera.

The city regularly attracts the world's leading stars from both East and West – and these acts draw large audiences from an increasing number of neighbouring countries. Over the years top international stars such as Aerosmith, Elton John, Mark Knopfler, Shakira, Sting and Robbie Williams have visited the Emirate and provided top-class concerts that have helped Dubai become the Gulf's leading entertainment centre.

This spread: Dubai International Airport is one of the fastest-growing airports in the world. Also under construction is a massive new international airport – Dubai World Central. Along with the new airport, the project will encompass several smaller 'cities' catering to various industries attached to aviation, including financial, industrial, services and tourism. It's estimated that the two airports will have the capacity to handle 190 million passengers a year, more than the populations of the UK, France and Italy combined.

Previous spread: The pace of construction round Dubai continues unabated. The expansion of the city's infrastructure is vital to meet the increasing needs of a burgeoning population and to satisfy Dubai's vision and desire to create an innovative, monumental city the world cannot fail to notice and admire.

While the Creek and the harbour at Hamriya provide wharfage for trading dhows, other vessels, including modern container ships and bulk carriers, require more sophisticated facilities such as those on offer at Port Rashid (above). Located close to the centre of the city, the port has a cruise-ship terminal for the ever-increasing amount of leisure ships that ply the Gulf.

The 71-berth Jebel Ali Port, the world's largest man-made harbour situated some 35 kilometres south-west of Dubai, is so large that it's visible from space. Jebel Ali has its own vast free zone – a hugely successful commercial and industrial area that provides companies with a range of benefits that include 100-per-cent-foreign ownership and a tax-free environment.

Dubai's maritime expertise has been expanded to include ship maintenance and repair. The Dubai Drydocks (left) is among the world's largest ship-repair yards. It has attracted business from more than 40 countries and can accommodate vessels of up to one million tonnes. Other yards on the Creek have facilities for smaller vessels and service oil-support tugs, dredgers and other craft. It is quite a contrast to see traditional trading dhows such as these (above) moored alongside modern containers and cranes.

A short trip from Dubai by car reveals an Arabia of a bygone era. Until relatively recently, many parts of the UAE could only be reached by camel. Now even remote areas have been made accessible by tarmac roads that slice across the desert and through the mountains. On the road to Hatta you'll pass towering dunes of red sand before encountering the stark landscape of the Hajar Mountains. Close to the road, you might even be lucky enough to discover a photogenic sandfall such as the one in an old quarry pictured here.

Surrounded by mountains, Hatta, a town some 90 minutes away from Dubai city centre, lies inland towards the east coast of the peninsula. It is thought to be one of the oldest inhabited places in the emirate, dating back some 3,000 years. The town is guarded by two round towers, and boasts some fascinating *falaj* (irrigation channels) nearby. Hatta's Heritage Village is well worth a visit and offers a glimpse into the lives of the peoples of ancient Arabia, with fully restored mud houses and date and palm-tree products similar to those that were once used on a daily basis.

For visitors who expect nothing but flat desert, the varied topography comes as something of a surprise. The mountain ridges are barren but beautiful, with picturesque villages deep in the valleys. In the wadis, gouged out by winter rains, trees maintain a precarious hold, while high above, the barren crests bake in the sun. And the dunefields themselves comprise many different landscapes, their colours varying from pale cream near the sea to deep red inland, dotted with gravel plains of varying sizes throughout. The height and form of the dunes change too, depending on the prevailing wind and the size and shape of the individual grains of sand.

Desert safaris, including dune-driving, quad-biking, sand-skiing, desert feasts and the chance to ride a camel, are popular activities on any tourist's itinerary. A ride on a camel is unforgettable; a smooth experience where the camel appears to glide over the sand. Dining in the warmth of a star-filled evening can be a smart or a casual affair, but Arabian hospitality is renowned throughout the world and your dining experience is likely to be of the highest standard, accompanied by a host of entertainment that could include a display of falconry or belly dancing.

This picturesque fort at Bithna, in the Emirate of Fujairah, stands guard over a strategically important wadi – Wadi Ham – which lies between Fujairah and the interior. Although the fort was built comparatively recently, evidence of human habitation in this area dates back some 4,000 years. The fort is nestled in among a luxuriant carpet of palm groves, which are watered by *aflaj*, a series of irrigation canals that channel the water to where it's needed, making the most of the precious natural resources the wadi affords.

On a rocky hill above a coastal plain stands Fujairah Fort, a stone and mud-brick edifice that sits on a site inhabited for thousands of years. Overlooking a large palm grove, old roofless mud huts of the original town lie at its feet. The castle was bombarded by the British Navy on April 20, 1925. The fort endured a 90-minute attack and received serious damage to its three sea-facing towers. Until recent renovations, evidence of this stood as a testament to the emirate's keen independence and undeniable spirit.

Fishing was, and still is, a fundamental part of life in the hot, arid Middle East and the warm waters of the Gulf and the East Coast provide an abundance of seafood, rich sources of nutrients that, in earlier times, were an essential part of the staple diet. The smaller fish are still used to produce cattle food and fertilizers.

Ideal for a weekend trip by 4x4 from Dubai, the Empty Quarter – or Rub al-Khali – is a vast wilderness area of dunes made famous by explorers such as Bertram Thomas, St John Philby and Wilfred Thesiger. It remains the place to enjoy the stillness and beauty of the desert, perhaps from an overnight camp.

The landscape of the Emirates, whether sand, gravel, rock, mountain, wadi, beach or mangrove, contains a variety of living creatures to reward the patient observer. The mix of reptiles includes 55 species and subspecies of snakes and a variety of lizards, one being the spiny tailed lizard known locally as the *dhub* (above). Spiders and scorpions (left) are not uncommon and best avoided when you come across them. Flamingoes (right top) and a variety of other birds may be seen in the mangroves (right bottom) of Dubai's wildlife sanctuary in Ra's al-Khor at the top end of the Creek. Bird lovers can watch the flamingoes from specially designed hides at the edge of the reserve.

An Arabian desert sunset is a wonderful sight and one difficult to replicate anywhere else in the world. The images on these two pages show one of the most traditional of Arabian scenes – a camel caravan progressing slowly and surely across the desert. Camels have been a mainstay of traditional Arab life since the dawn of time. Regarded as God's gift to the Bedouin, these ships of the desert are exceptionally suited to their harsh environment. Prior to the advent of the faster but less efficient motor vehicle, they provided a means of transport to their owners, sport in the form of camel-racing, and sustenance from their milk and meat. Nothing was wasted. If a camel was slaughtered to celebrate a wedding or other special occasion, their hides, bones and hair were used to make bags, utensils and garments.

To cater for the anticipated increase in the numbers of residents and visitors to Dubai, development continues with projects such as the three palm islands, The World, Dubai Marina, Dubai Waterfront and Dubailand. Towering over all of these will be Burj Dubai, the world's tallest building. The project is part of the biggest single construction site the world has ever seen.

Also under way is the Dubai Metro (left), which will introduce railroad commuting to the city, with first-class compartments as well as those for women and children. Dubai Festival City (below) is a vast residential, shopping and golfing complex taking shape next to the Creek.

Business Bay (above) is a leading international commercial and business cluster located along an extended Dubai Creek from Ra's al-Khor to Sheikh Zayed Road. Offshore, property on Dubai's three palm-shaped islands and on The World, a 300-island archipelago, are available to purchase on a freehold basis and represent the ultimate in exclusive island living. The palm islands include The Palm Deira (left top) and the The Palm Jebel Ali (left bottom). Abutting The Palm Jebel Ali, the Dubai Waterfront is the first stage of a far larger project that includes the 75-kilometre Arabian Canal.

Meydan is a new horseracing complex that will feature sand and turf tracks, a kilometre-long grandstand, a hotel, restaurants, the Godolphin Gallery, a museum, covered parking for 10,000 cars and a four-kilometre canal which will run from Dubai Creek to the racecourse. During the off-season the grandstand will serve as a dining, business and conference facility.

To accompany the record-breaking Burj Dubai, the Dubai Mall will be the world's largest shopping mall, covering an area equivalent to the size of more than 50 football pitches. This magnificent destination will come replete with aquaria filled with sharks and stingrays that can be viewed from tunnels, as well as an artificial lake and the world's largest gold souk.

Acknowledgements

The publishers would like to thank all the photographers
who supplied images for this book. Our thanks also go to the
Dubai Chamber of Commerce & Industry
for their invaluable support and encouragement.

PHOTOGRAPHIC CREDITS

Arabian Ranches Golf Club: 92B
Crowell, Charles: 51
Dubai Creek Golf & Yacht Club: 93
Dubai Duty Free: 98, 109
Dubai Festival City: 139B
Dubai Holding: 141
Dubai Ports World: 116, 117
Emaar Properties: 138, 143
Emirates airline: 15T&B, 48, 115, 136/137
Gallo/Getty Images: 96
Jumeirah: 84, 136
Lichfield, Patrick: 134T
Meydan/TDF: 142
Milne-Home, Bob: 32
Motivate Publishing: 46BL&BR, 66, 97TL&TR, 97B
Adiseshan, Shankar: 13, 99R, 114, 126
Duncan Chard: 2, 46TR,
Gwanny, Fadi: 119
Jackson, Warren: 45
Kita, Karel: Front cover, 60, 66, 80B
Newington, Greg: 34, 49
Pereira, Sheldon: 40, 46TL
Salik, Farooq: 95, 111
Walsh, Callaghan: 69, 74, 75, 99L
Nakheel: 140T, 140B
Nowell, John: 130
One&Only Royal Mirage: 76/77, 77
Dubai Roads and Transport Authority: 139T
Sanderson, Pippa: 35, 41, 42, 47, 62, 63, 67, 68, 81, 85, 92T, 118, 123, Back cover
Steele, David: 4/5, 6/7, 9, 10, 11, 12, 14, 18, 18/19, 21T&B, 24, 25T&B, 31, 36, 37, 38/39,
44TL&TR, 54, 55, 56/57, 58/59, 61, 64, 65, 70, 71, 72/73, 78T, 78/79, 80T, 86/87,
88/89, 89, 90, 91, 94/95, 100, 101, 102, 103, 104, 105T, 105B, 106/107, 108,
110, 112/113, 120/121, 122, 124/125, 128, 129, 131, 132/133, 134B, 135T, 135B
White, Aaron: 78B
Willmore, Andrea: 1, 8, 16, 16/17, 20T&B, 22T&B, 23T, 23BL&BR, 26, 27, 28, 28/29, 30, 33, 39,
44BL&BR, 50T&B, 52/53, 57, 82, 83
Zandi, Dariush: 43

T: top; B: bottom; L: left; R: right